To Jeanne —
with much love —
xx
Karen Taylor-Good

On Angel's Wings

Messages & Songs
Of
Inspiration & Hope

by Karen Taylor-Good

On Angel's Wings

by
Karen Taylor-Good

Published by:
Insight Publications, Ltd.
P. O Box 25066
Nashville, Tennessee 37202
(615) 228-8060
taylor@karentaylorgood.com

ISBN 0-9725906-0-9

Editor/Layout: **Olivia Cloud**
Editorial: **Pam Grau**
Photographs of Karen By: **Nancy Lee Andrews**
—www.portfolios.com/Nancy Lee Andrews
Cover Photograph By: **Jim De Lutes** — www.jdlphotos.com
Cover Design By: **guerrilla designs** — www.guerrilladesign.com

About the Companion CD

You can read the book on its own and then listen to the CD at another time, or — read the stories, then listen to the corresponding song. You can follow along with the lyrics as you listen, or just close your eyes and let the songs speak to you.

About the Blank Pages

We've added some blank pages so that you can use them to write down any thoughts and feelings that the stories, songs, and love notes may evoke.

Contents

The "On Angel's Wings" CD is at the end of the book.

Kudos for Karen

"Beautiful! Courageous! Rare! Inspired! I would ask what planet Karen Taylor-Good is from, but I know earth produces people like her once in a blue moon, to show the rest of us what it means to be fully human."

Chris Livingston
Screenwriter and Director — **New York, NY**

"I saw you for the first time on the Home Shopping Network the other night. I am a minister and I noticed a very distinct anointing on your music and voice that only comes from God. Not just a good voice, or a good keyboard player, but a supernatural talent gift specifically from God to help and heal people's hearts."

Rev. James Derrick Horne,
Minister — **Huntsville, AL**

"At the Kerrville Folk Festival I heard you sing "On Angel's Wings." Karen, I absolutely broke down in tears. I wept harder than I did when I heard Dad had died. Believe me when I tell you that crying in public is not something that comes naturally to me. I wanted you to know that there is a special place in my heart for your music, especially "On Angel's Wings." No other song has ever had the same emotional impact on me."

Gary Trobridge — Plano, TX

"Karen's music soothes my soul. I find her word touching and her melodies and beautiful voice the balm I need in times of stress. She values the humanness in us all and portrays it so beautifully!"

Janet L. Jones
CEO, Alive Hospice **— Nashville, TN**

"When you sang 'Real,' it touched me so deeply . . . I was amazed that someone put into words how I've been feeling all my life."

Kathy Compton — Hazelwood, MO

"Karen Taylor-Good can say more in a four-minute song than I can pack into a 20-minute talk. Karen's message is powerful and full of love, and we are always delighted when she's in Dallas."

Rev. Ellen Debenport
Associate Minister **— Dallas, TX**

"I'll never forget hearing "Precious Child" for the first time. Even though it had been years since our daughter was killed, the tears were flowing just as hard as if it had been two days since she died. I think what Karen does is so powerful."

Mary Bell
Program Chair, The Compassionate Friends **— Chicago, IL**

"I cannot tell you how much your songs have touched my heart. The power of your music literally moved mountains in my life, and gave me the power to lift the dead weight of the giant shame from my life."

Arionnah Isabela Powell
Founder, Honor Thy Children —- **Sheboygan, WI**

"Karen Taylor-Good's music opens pathways like no other! She brings a sound that creates emotional honesty and allows listeners to go to those so hard to reach places. Karen understands that it is your pain that leads you through the caverns of your heart into true joy. Experience the feeling!"

Nancy Joy Hefron
Heartlight Imagery — **Mount Vernon, IA**

"We use your music because it speaks so clearly to the struggle we may feel in being more real. Music will often convey a message that spoken words cannot, and your songs — both in how they are sung and in what they say — share those messages simply, clearly and deeply."

Sue Muck
Newton Learning Corporation — **San Diego, CA**

"Karen is our congregation's favorite guest and teacher. She afflicts the comfortable and comforts the afflicted. Karen is a real, vulnerable, dynamic, strong woman with a message the world needs right now."

Rev. Barbara Clevenger
Senior Minister — **Detroit, MI**

Acknowledgments

My love and heartfelt thanks to **Taylor Sparks** — manager supremo, cheerleader, mentor, friend, teacher — for encouraging me to write this book, and for the countless hours you've spent editing, typing, plotting and planning.

To: **Doug Grau** — for your wise counsel.

To: **Ta Kimble** — for your sharp eye, and gentle heart.

To: **Pam Grau** — for punctuation, grammar and dot-dot-dot removal help!

To: **Jason Blume** — for wonderful rewrite suggestions and your precious friendship.

To: **Jerry Vandiver** — for great advice and generous sharing of knowledge.

To: **Jhesi Boyer** — for all your help and energy.

To: My sister **Bonnie** — I love you dearly,

To: My brother **Raoul** and sister **Brenda** — I love and appreciate you so much.

To: **Merri Feirman** — for your friendship, love and continued support.

To: **Chris Olson** — for teaching me about football and friendship.

To: **my sweet parents and my precious child** — thank you for allowing me to share stories about you. You each mean so very much to me and I love you more than I can say.

Special thanks to my husband, **Dennis** — thank you for being my toughest critic, for suggesting the "Love Notes," and for loving me through my crazies.

Foreword

I first witnessed Karen's awesome musical talent in 1999. She was doing the "special music" at a church service in Atlanta. She sang "Healing in the Hands of Time" and "Real." My wife, JoAnna, and I were immediately hooked! We bought all her CDs and listened to everything she had ever written and recorded.

We found her lyrics so in alignment with my teachings on Radical Forgiveness and spirituality, and her rendering of the songs so sensitive and heart opening, that we have used her music in all our workshops ever since. Sometimes we are even blessed to have her perform live at major events.

Her ability to help people get in touch with their feelings and to fully connect with the healer within is extraordinary. Her lyrics touch people's souls directly and she heals through her voice. I believe that as you listen to Karen's music you will experience a healing too. Your heart will open and your soul will be touched.

Knowing also, through reading this book, how Karen came to write these wonderful songs will deepen the experience and remind you of your own beautiful life stories — and perhaps some that were not so beautiful. Like all of us, Karen is a wounded healer. When we share our wounds with each other we evoke the healer in each other. Through her songs, all created out of her life experience, Karen has elevated this to an art form that can only be described as divinely inspired.

For me, what I like so much about her songs is that even if they evoke sorrow or grief, they inspire us to see beyond the pain and to feel the love that flows behind the apparent circumstances of our lives. Her songs always leave you feeling uplifted and much more fully connected with the Divine than before. That's what makes us want to listen to them over and over again. Karen is great therapy for the soul!

I am truly blessed to have Karen Taylor-Good as my friend.

Colin Tipping, Author
RADICAL Forgiveness

Preface

When I first discovered that I was a songwriter, I was thrilled. Music had always been such a big part of my life, and now here I was, able to turn my thoughts and fears and joys and worries into song! I wrote about my depression and confusion about my life's path. I wrote about my sadness and fear as I was getting a divorce. I wrote about my daughter, morphing from a sweet, dear child into some angst-filled adolescent I didn't recognize. I wrote about my parents, changing from the pillars of strength I had leaned on all my life to two sweet, elderly souls who very much needed to lean on me.

I began to write with other people, and sometimes we wrote to exorcise their demons, sometimes mine.

It was cathartic. It was intense. It was magic. "Thank you God!!" What a terrific gift! I knew that I would always be able to help my own little soul to cope in this gentle, powerful, musical way. I never dreamed that my words and my music would touch other souls. I am honored.

May this book and CD bring you comfort. May it help you find tears, and laughter, and a remembrance that you are not alone.

We are all in this life adventure together. If my words and my songs can help ease your way in this wondrous, puzzling, often difficult journey, then I have accomplished what I was put here to do.

Thank you for opening your heart.
Karen Taylor-Good

Unanswered Prayers

I feel very blessed indeed to be doing what I love to do — writing songs that matter to me, singing them myself, and putting them out to the world to do good. I have discovered my gift. Finally!! — It did take me a while.

I always knew that I had been given the gift of a good singing voice. "Okay then," said I in my early twenties, "I'll be in Holiday Inn® cover bands, singing "Proud Mary'" to really drunk people until two in the morning! THAT must be what I'm supposed to do with this gift!" Well, it didn't take me too long to figure out — that wasn't quite right!

In my mid-twenties, I moved to Memphis, and I began to use my voice in a different way. I punched a time card at

8:30 in the morning, and I went into the studio and sang whatever was put in front of me — "KELP . . . El Paso!" and "WSIX . . . Nashville!" and endless jingles touting dog food, toilet paper, etc. etc. — until 3:30 in the afternoon, when I punched out. It felt a little more right than the Holiday Inn® gigs, but not much.

I turned 30. Nashville was right down the road. "Okay! I'll bet I'm supposed to be a country music star!" I forgot to ask myself some pertinent questions — like, Karen, do you really want to be a country music star? Do you want to be on a bus 285 days a year? Do you like singing songs that other people write for you? (But, I had no choice, for I had not been chosen to be a writer of songs. That gift was reserved for The Few, The Blessed — The Truly Talented.)

Four years and ten nationally-charted country radio singles later, I was actually nominated for an Academy of Country Music Award — Best New Female Artist! Ah, at last!

This would be it! This was why I had been given a voice. I was supposed to sing other people's songs and get played on the radio and be cute and sexy and FAMOUS. I went to a psychic. She told me I was going to win! I went out to L.A. There I was among the stars. This is it! Here goes! Live. Network TV. I did my performance. I went backstage. I waited to hear my name called! "And the winner is — Nicolette Larson!!!" Oh no. This just can't be.

This was MY award. This was MY path. What happened? What went wrong? I spiraled down into a deep dark depression which lasted for months and months. "Thanks a lot, God," I cried. "You gave me this voice and I've tried and tried to figure out why, but nothing I do works out." I was hurting so deeply that I had to do something. I needed to express what I was feeling. I needed to write it down. I wrote. And I wrote. And I wrote. Then, I began to read what I was writing, and I wondered — could it be? I crept over to the piano in the dark of one night, writings in hand, and I nervously, cautiously put my hands to the keyboard. The music came pouring out. The words turned into song lyrics. I sang MY words, about what was in MY heart, set to MY music. And the world came into focus, and I knew why I was here.

I'm getting better, every day, at trusting that there really is a Plan, and that even though I have no idea what it looks like — Somebody clearly does.

"What I Need"

by Karen Taylor-Good & Jason Blume

I knew all the answers, the way my life should go
When I used to say my prayers, I would tell God so
It seemed He wasn't listening, I thought He didn't care
But looking back it's plain to see, He was always there

'Cause I prayed for strength
And I got pain that made me strong
I prayed for courage
And got fear to overcome
When I prayed for faith
My empty heart brought me to my knees
I don't always get what I want
I get what I need

I'm not saying that it's easy, or that it doesn't hurt
When nothing seems to go my way, nothing seems to work
But these days I'm getting better at going with the flow
Accepting that sometimes, the answer to a prayer is "no"

'Cause I prayed for strength
And I got pain that made me strong
I prayed for courage
And got fear to overcome
When I prayed for faith
My empty heart brought me to my knees
I don't always get what I want
I get what I need

Every time I've had a door slammed in my face
In time a better one was opened in its place

I prayed for strength
And I got pain that made me strong
I prayed for courage
And got fear to overcome
When I prayed for faith
My empty heart brought me to my knees
I don't always get what I want
I get what I need

Love Note

If you are feeling battered and bruised from all of the doors slamming shut in front of you — hang in there. Those doors are closing for a reason! You are a precious child of God, and you are being pushed, nudged, and guided toward your Destiny.

Hold the Mayo

I could be the poster child for the "Sandwich Generation" — those of us who are lucky enough to still have our parents alive, and needing us, and who are lucky enough to have children alive, and needing us. And there we are, sandwiched in between — lucky, blessed, needed, pulled, stressed and exhausted. I'm not complaining, I swear. Well, okay, maybe I am — but just a little. They all enrich my life and bring me great pleasure and love. And on a good day, that's all I can see. Then there are days like yesterday.

I had taken my father to the hospital emergency room the day before. He was having trouble breathing. Now, he's in for a few days as they treat him for pneumonia and look at his amazing, frail 89 year-old heart to see if they can help it beat any stronger. I had just picked up my mom, who was particularly agitated and worried and having a very hard time remembering things after having spent a night without my dad. We were on our way to the hospital and I was doing my best to calm my mama down, when my cell phone rang. It was my daughter Rachael. She was 45 minutes away at her boyfriend's house, on the floor, writhing in pain, crying, scared to death, experiencing severe abdominal pains, and needing her Mommy. Well then! They say that "God never gives us more than we can handle." I was seconds away from tossing up my hands and yelling, "HELLO??? THIS IS WAY TOO HARD!! I QUIT!!

I didn't. I took a deep breath, and began to perform an amazing job (if I do say so myself) of mothering, daughtering, and juggling. Drive, calm down the child, stop at a light, look up the doctor's number. Drive, calm down the mother, stop at a light, call Rachael's boss and tell him she won't be in to work. Drive. Call the doctor's office, have them call

Rachael so she can tell them her symptoms. Drive. Calm down the mother. Calm down the child. Call Rachael's boyfriend, instruct him to go buy the proper medicine. Drive. Reach the hospital. Deliver the mother to the father's room. Visit. Talk with the doctors re: his condition. Check with daughter re: her condition.

I remind myself that I have a sister and a husband, and I don't have to do everything by myself! Leave parents at hospital with sister. Call husband to take over with daughter. Go attend to my own life and my own business for two hours. Back to hospital. Visit. Calm. Nurture. Reassure. Drive the mother back to her home, drive myself home. Collapse into a lifeless heap, cry, search for chocolate, give thanks for a strong constitution and great juggling skills. My life is full. I am blessed. And I'm not complaining. Well — maybe just a little.

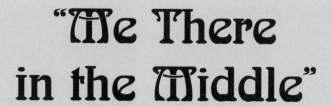

"Me There in the Middle"

by Karen Taylor-Good & Lisa Silver

Dear God I've drawn this picture to make it crystal clear
I feel the need to show you why I'm praying hard down here
On the left there stand the very ones,
the ones who gave me life
The one that I gave birth to, is standing on my right
That's me there in the middle, two arms stretched out wide
Holding on for dear life, being pulled from side to side

Give me strength, help me be the rock
Give me patience, 'cause they've all become my flock
Give me courage, as they change please help me know
You'll give me the strength to hold them
And the strength ... to let them go

I know you're watching over them, I'm not in it by myself
But it's taking all the faith I have, I need some extra help
Mom & Dad are awfully frail, and getting more confused

My 15-year-old knows it all, and hasn't got a clue
And me there in the middle, both sides leaning hard
They need all my energy, I need a stronger heart

Give me strength, help me be the rock
Give me patience, 'cause they've all become my flock
Give me courage, as they change please help me know
You'll give me the strength to hold them
And the strength ... to let them go

Who made me the grown up?
I don't know which scares me more
Watching Dad behind the wheel
Or my child head out the door

Give me strength, help me be the rock
Give me patience, 'cause they've all become my flock
Give me courage, as they change please help me know
You'll give me the strength to hold them
And the strength...to let them go

Love Note

If you are the meat in a multi-generational sand-wich, or in any situation in which others are relying on you, my heart is with you. This is not easy stuff. Please remember what they tell you when you get on the airplane. "Put YOUR oxygen mask on FIRST — then take care of the people who need you." So rest. Exercise. Find a support group. Talk to loving friends. You'll be a better care-giver for it.

Flight Preparations

My mother is a Leo. She belongs to MENSA (the organization for people with genius I.Q.s). She has been a FORCE in my life — a huge presence — the center of my family — my rock — my foundation. She is now 87 years old. (She still lies about her age — to the doctor, to the government — tells them that she's 82!) In the past, if I had to use one word to describe her, it would be SHARP; in every way, with every one of her senses — SHARP.

I remember clearly the day I discovered that she would not always be my sharp, together mama. My folks were visiting from El Paso, prior to moving here, and I was struck by how much eyesight my mom had lost since the last time I was with her. (She is legally blind from macular degeneration.) Still, she wanted some paper to write stories on the plane ride home. I brought her a legal pad, and as she took it from me, she grabbed it wrong and got a paper cut on her finger. "Ouch!" she said. "I cut my finger!" "Gosh, do you want a Band-Aid®?" I asked. "No," she answered, "I'm ok." Then I went out in the hall to get some more things together, and two minutes later, she came out and said, "Karen ... do you have a Band-Aid®? I don't know what I did to my finger." Uh oh. There I was, standing in my hall, and I literally felt the earth shake.

THIS CANNOT BE HAPPENING. I kept it together long enough to get them on the plane, and then I went to pieces. "God ... what is this??? This stinks. Why are you doing this? Please don't! This is so unkind. This is downright mean." I begged and pleaded. I shouted and railed. I cried and I cried. I decided that it was a one-time incident and would never happen again. I was wrong.

The last four years have been quite a journey, for my mother and for me. What I have come to believe is that God is being very kind, indeed. My mother's ties to this earth have been incredibly strong. She has lived a very long lifetime, relying on her intellect, her mind, her "knowledge." My mom's favorite quote as she has gotten older is from Dylan Thomas — "Do not go gentle into that good night." She does NOT want to leave here! She has no belief in a life after this one — in a loving God — or any God at all. How is this precious, earth-bound soul ever going to loosen her ties to this life enough to let go and make her transition to the next?

Ah, God works in mysterious ways.

"On Angel's Wings"

by Karen Taylor-Good & Jason Blume

This is the woman who had all the answers
The one I would lean on for comfort, for strength
She's never forgotten one grandchild's birthday
Now she can't remember my name
And it makes me so angry, I shake my fist
And cry out to the heavenly one
Why would you play such a cold-hearted trick?
I thought your job was to love
And the answer came down from above:

She's gonna fly
When her time here is through
First she'll have to let go
Of some things she can't use
'Cause people and places, memories and faces
Are just way too heavy, it seems
To carry on angel's wings

This is the woman who saw things so clearly
The one who could pick out one crumb on the floor
She saw through a white lie, saw me through love's eyes
She hardly can see anymore
And it makes me so sad, and it just isn't fair
Why should so much be taken away?
But when I cry out for all that she's lost
I silently hear someone say

She's gonna fly
When her time here is through
First she'll have to let go
Of some things she can't use
'Cause people and places, memories and faces
Are just way too heavy, it seems
To carry on angel's wings
And OH! ... the wonders she'll see
And I know she'll remember to watch over me

She's gonna fly
When her time here is through
First she'll have to let go
Of some things she can't use
'Cause people and places, memories and faces
Are just way too heavy, it seems
To carry on angel's wings

Love Note

If you are going through a difficult time with one of your parents now — if you have become the parent, and they the child — if they are "not who they were," and you find yourself confused, stressed, and angry, I understand. I know this is NOT easy. And it's alright, and it's perfect.

Breathe. Cry. Go to a ridiculous movie. Take a walk. Find a support group. Consume moderate amounts of chocolate. Take good care of yourself. My heart is with you.

The Not So
Still Small Voice

It was 1991, and I had given up a lucrative career singing national radio and TV commercials in Memphis, Nashville, and Chicago. It had become painfully obvious that making big bucks trying to get people to buy this particular brand of peanut butter or fly that particular airline was not feeding my soul. I knew that I was a songwriter now, and that I was supposed to be writing songs! But when I showed them around in Nashville, absolutely nobody cared!! (My favorite joke — How do you get a songwriter's attention in Nashville? — "Oh, waiter!")

Yes, it seemed that EVERYBODY in Nashville was writing songs, and everybody was trying to get noticed. My bank account had dwindled down to a dangerously low point, and I had been to see a bankruptcy attorney. One Sunday morning when the alarm went off, I was just too depressed and feeling too sorry for myself, so I turned off the alarm and said, "Forget it. I'm sleeping in." So, I hear this little bitty voice, and it says — "Go to church!" And I say, "no way." And then the voice gets a little bit louder — "Go to church!" And I put a pillow over my head. And the voice gets a LOT louder and says — "GO TO CHURCH!!!" And although I wasn't at all happy about it, I figured I'd better go!

The minister gave an amazing talk that morning about saying "YES!" to life, and about how often we all say "No." And he challenged us to take a pledge and to say "YES" to life as often as we could, just for a week. I was jazzed; I was inspired. I took the pledge! Right after the service was over, this woman I hardly knew walked up to me and said, "Karen, you're a songwriter . . . . I have this friend coming to town, and he's an actor from L.A., and he's just started writing songs, so, will you write with him?" Oh man, you should have heard the committee that lives in my mind go off on that one! "Oh my God, he's an actor from L.A.! He's probably the biggest jerk around, and I'm sure he's got a huge ego, and he's not even a real songwriter yet, blah, blah, blah . . . ." I promise you that there is NO WAY I ever would have said yes. However . . . I had just taken . . . the PLEDGE!!!

I was not happy. I gritted my teeth and eeked out a "yes," figuring that I would have this egotistical jerk over for coffee and then dismiss him. Can you see what's coming here? Enter Burton Collins . . . nice guy, actor, screenwriter, good songwriter. As we drank our coffee, he shared that he had been very close to his grandmother, and was with her when she was dying. He told me that his grandma saw what a hard time he was having, and that she looked at him and asked,

"Burton, how can I help you say goodbye?" He asked me if I thought that would make a good song. Oh my. Did I! We wrote the song in a few hours, and my life was changed forever. The song was recorded by Patty Loveless and went to number one on the Country charts. It was nominated for many awards, including a Grammy®. It also was recorded by Al Jarreau, Laura Branigan, several European artists, and continues to be found on karaoke machines everywhere! I got a wonderful publishing deal, and am living in the house that "How Can I Help You Say Goodbye" built.

I thank God for pushing me out of bed on that fateful Sunday!

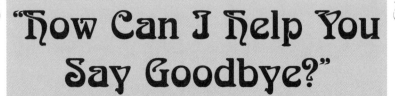

"How Can I Help You Say Goodbye?"

by Karen Taylor-Good & Burton Banks Collins

Through the back window of our fifty-nine wagon
I watched my best friend Jamie slipping further away
I kept on waving till I couldn't see her
Then through my tears I asked again why we couldn't stay
Mama whispered softly, time will ease your pain
Life's about changing, nothing ever stays the same and she said

How can I help you to say goodbye?
It's ok to hurt and it's ok to cry
Come let me hold you and I will try
How can I help you to say goodbye?

I sat on our bed, he packed his suitcase
I held a picture of our wedding day
His hands were trembling, we both were crying
He kissed me gently, then he quickly walked away
I called up Mama, she said, time will ease your pain
Life's about changing, nothing ever stays the same and she said

How can I help you to say goodbye?
It's ok to hurt and it's ok to cry
Come let me hold you and I will try
How can I help you to say goodbye?

Sitting with Mama, alone in her bedroom
She opened her eyes and then squeezed my hand
She said, I have to go now, my time here is over
And with her final words she tried to help me understand
Mama whispered softly, time will ease your pain
Life's about changing, nothing ever stays the same and she said

How can I help you to say goodbye?
It's ok to hurt and it's ok to cry
Come let me hold you and I will try
How can I help you to say goodbye?

Love Note

Listen to the "still small/loud voice" when it speaks to you — and perhaps especially on those days when you want to hide under the covers and/or stick your head in the sand. Be brave, come on out to play, and say "YES" to life!

Second
Love Note

I believe that this song deserves two. I said "good-bye" to my precious 89 and 87 year-old parents a few days ago. I put them on a plane, and they flew 1,500 miles away, to live with my brother and sister-in-law, after having lived one mile from me for the last three years. My heart is really aching. I never understood that expression before — but I do now. I feel lost and empty, and I can't stop crying. So this love note is for me, as well as for those of you who have had to say

41

"goodbye." When we love deeply and then lose people, the hurt that we feel is a blessed pain. It allows us to know that we are fully human. Breathe through the hurt. Love yourself for being able to feel it.

Remember that saying goodbye is part of the journey, and that we will greet each other once again, on this side, or on the other. And, it really does hurt. And, it's really ok.

The Shnoz and I

I did not have a horrible childhood. I had a stable home, a mother and a father who loved me dearly, a couple of siblings, fairly normal stuff. I was a really pretty baby — blonde hair, blue eyes, and the cutest little nose. I was a really pretty toddler — blonde hair, blue eyes, and there was that little nose.

First grade, second, all the way to sixth, and I was just still darn cute! In seventh grade, I was co-leader of the cheerleading squad at Putnam Elementary in El Paso. I was confident and happy, although my hair was getting browner and duller, and whoa — what WAS going on there in the middle of my face? Something happened to me during the summer between seventh and eighth grade. This thing that was once a cute little button variety had turned into a HONKER. Oh my. It was big. It was crooked.

First day of eighth grade — new school — high school. Tryouts for cheerleader. Every one of my friends from the Putnam squad made it — except for me. I was devastated. Shortly afterwards, there appeared a mean, overweight, loud-mouthed boy who became my tormentor. He would spot me, at least once a day, and he would yell out, "HEY BEAK!!!!!" I would cringe. I would hide. I wanted to die. Eighth grade, ninth grade, tenth grade. I was a shy, unhappy kid. I hated the way I looked. I hated that boy.

My life could have gone down the tubes right then. I could have retreated into myself. I could have become filled with anger and resentment at the bullies of this world, and my own bully in particular. I could have searched for retribution. I could have been lost. As Fate would have it, I found my salvation in the choir in eleventh grade. I discovered that I had something special — a gift — and it changed me at my core. I could not be totally ugly if I had a beautiful voice. I began to carry myself different-ly. I began to see myself differently. My tormentor moved on to torture weaker prey.

Fast forward 30 some years. I am a grown woman. My nose has been long replaced with a smaller model. I am a mother. I have a beautiful daughter who is teased unmercifully. I am once again shocked and saddened by how very cruel children can be. Where I turned to music for escape, Rachael turned to drugs and alcohol. We were fortunate to find a high school especially for kids dealing with their addictions. There, she and all of the other kids did a lot of work on their self-esteem issues, on dealing with peer pressure, and coping with adolescence.

April 20, 1999. Littleton, Colorado. Columbine High School. Two teased, tormented and bullied boys have finally had enough. They don't have the choir to turn to. They don't find a different kind of school where they can talk about their feelings and frustrations. The only thing they can think of to ease their pain is revenge — and violence.

A year later, the father of one of the slain girls came to Nashville and gave a most amazing and insightful talk. His message: "My daughter would be ALIVE today if we could simply teach our children to be KINDER."

We must.

"Kinder"

by Karen Taylor-Good & Jason Blume

She sits alone in a corner of the lunchroom
They call her names as they walk by
She acts like she doesn't care,
but there's so much pain in there
She holds it back so they won't see her cry . . .
Could we be

Kinder, a little blinder
To the differences that get in our way
'Cause when we're kinder, that's God's reminder
That in His eyes, we're really all the same

He's the one nobody wants on their team
'Cause he's so different from the rest
And they tease him every day, they call him "freak"
they call him "gay"
Do they feel more by making him feel less? . . .
Could we be

Kinder, a little blinder
To the differences that get in our way
'Cause when we're kinder, that's God's reminder
That in His eyes, we're really all the same

An open heart, an open hand
That's where it starts
We can take a stand . . . and just be
Kinder, a little blinder
To the differences that get in our way
'Cause when we're kinder, that's God's reminder
That in His eyes, we're really all the same.
We're really all the same
Could we be kinder?

Love Note

It is so painful to watch your child being treated unkindly, and equally painful if your child is the perpetrator. If your child is dealing with bullying issues, from either side, please get help for them.

(See "People Helping People" at the end of this book.)

Superman Unplugged

Several years ago, I attended a truly incredible, life-changing week of "co-dependency treatment." It was a week where twelve complete strangers came together (six male, six female), and with the help of some caring and insightful therapists, we began to explore, together, what made us tick. We recreated our families of origin, playing key roles for each other, acting out the parts. It was an amazing adventure.

Every one of us, by week's end, was able to reach some very deep, painful places. I was struck by one startling fact: it took the men an awful lot longer to get to their feelings, and to let them show. We all discovered, together, that they had been trained and conditioned to be strong, to hold everything in, and above all — NOT to cry.

By the end of the week, a miracle occurred. These very men who had been so stiff, tight, and carefully masked were holding teddy bears and crying like babies. I had never seen a more beautiful sight. I was deeply moved by their struggle, by their honesty, and by their bravery.

"Real Men Cry"

by Karen Taylor-Good & Taylor Sparks

I know that you've heard all your life
Emotions make men weak
You must be brave you must be bold
And tears are for the meek
And so you've held it all inside
Like you were taught to do
But your soul feels like it's dying
It's time to tell the truth

Real men cry, real men feel
Real men are not made of steel
And real men hurt, in spite of what you've learned
Believe me it's no lie . . . real men cry

Forget what you were told to be
Just be the things you are
A man of passion, fire and dreams
Who listens to his heart
A man who doesn't hide himself
Behind a wall of stone

And shows the world he's human
Made of tears and flesh and bone

Real men cry, real men feel
Real men are not made of steel
And real men hurt, in spite of what you've learned
Believe me it's no lie . . . real men cry

After a lifetime of pretending
What you knew was never true
You can write a brand new story
It's time to be the real you

Real men cry, real men feel
Real men are not made of steel
And real men hurt, in spite of what you've learned
Believe me it's no lie . . . real men cry

Love Note

Dear precious child of God, living this lifetime in a male body. Your path is a difficult one. So much is expected of you. Your tears are hard won. They are beautiful and special. Let them flow.

The Wisdom of Pinocchio

I had seen the movie "Pinocchio" when I was a child. Several times. Back then I thought it was a cute little story about a wooden boy. Years later, as an adult, and one who had been a 'performer' forever, I saw Pinocchio again. I was astounded. I was dumbfounded. I was profoundly moved. You see, I TOO was tired of being a puppet — "pulled by invisible strings." I was exhausted by the constant effort of performing — and not just performing to make my living. Performing for everyone. I was playing the part of a cool, aloof, hip, chick singer, when in truth I still carried a mental picture of myself as that gawky, buck-toothed, big-nosed kid, and I was terrified that the world would find me out for the phony I was.

I was playing the part of a successful studio singer and was making good money, but I never believed that I deserved it. I figured somebody was making a mistake, and eventually they would figure it out. I was pretty much living in a state of constant fear, and not acknowledging it — to myself or to anyone else. Quite an unpleasant way to live. Then, bit by bit, workshop by workshop, therapist by therapist, self-help book by self-help book, 12-step meeting by 12-step meeting, I began to get in touch with all the fear and hurt and anger and frustration that was living inside of me, and little by little, I was willing to let other people see it, too. At last, I could cry when I was hurting, I could scream when I was angry, I could be ridiculous and sweaty and smelly and inappropriate and sexy and not-sexy and cool and not-so cool.

Recently, I attended a Champions on Ice show, featuring many of the Olympic skaters we've all come to know so well. I found several glaring and beautiful metaphors on the subject of being "Real." One skater in particular won the crowd's heart. He had quite obviously decided that he was

VERY comfortable with and proud of who he was, and he proceeded to show us an aspect of his personality that was flamboyant and outrageous! He was precious as he skated in all his sequined glory to "In the Navy" and then segued into "YMCA." The audience ADORED him. He was totally REAL.

The next skater had won many awards, medals, and championships. We all had seen him do quadruple jumps on TV, and yet this night he was very reserved and didn't seem to be "going for it." It was as if he was playing it safe to be sure he didn't fall and embarrass himself. The audience, myself included, responded very coolly. The NEXT skater who came out went for it in every moment. He ended up missing a jump and he landed quite unceremoniously on his behind in front of 10,000 people. He then sprawled out on his back, as if to say, "Oh well!" The audience, myself included, went WILD!!! It wasn't a failure. It was somebody daring to be real and human and make mistakes, and to fall on his rear end in the process! I want to do the same.

"Real"

by Karen Taylor-Good & Angela Kaset

Last night I saw that movie
The one about the wooden boy
The good news is he could feel no sadness
The bad news is he could feel no joy
And it hit me hard ... a puppet on a shelf
So when he wished on a far off star
You know I made that same wish for myself . . . .
I wanna be real . . . real
Drop the act, take off the mask and feel . . . real

Well I've been going through the motions
Pulled by invisible strings
And I've pushed down the hurt and I've held back the tears
And covered up the dreams
But beneath it all . . . trying hard to breathe
The Me I buried long ago
Is screaming to break free
I wanna be real . . . real
Drop the act, take off the mask and feel . . . real

Let the fear go, let the heart show
Let the world see me . . . I wanna be real

And goodbye wooden heart
Goodbye painted smile

I wanna dance in a crowd, I wanna laugh out loud
I wanna act like a fool, I wanna be uncool
I wanna cry when I hurt, I wanna sweat when I work
I want help when I fall, I wanna feel it, feel it all
I wanna be real

Take off the mask . . . be real
Let my heart show . . . real
I wanna be real

Love Note

If you've been wearing a mask — hiding who you really are; if you've been proceeding very carefully through life, so you won't fall, 'fail', or make a fool of yourself — I understand, perfectly. AND, I invite you to come on out and play with those of us who are ditching the masks, being real, and sometimes falling on our butts! It doesn't hurt nearly as much as hiding does. I promise.

Speaking the Unspeakable

This is a difficult subject to write about. It's a difficult subject to talk about. It makes us uncomfortable. It's so awful. It's so evil. Thank God I did not experience this kind of abuse as a child, but several of my dearest friends did. It's so much easier to just ignore it and look the other way. But ignoring the devastating effect that physical, emotional and sexual abuse has on a child's psyche is the worst thing we can do. It taints the way a person feels about themselves and the way they respond to life.

It is the SILENCE surrounding child abuse that gives it power. We need to SHOUT from the rooftops, "THIS IS NOT OKAY!" "THIS IS NOT ACCEPTABLE!!"

The wounds go very deep, and they last a lifetime. There was surely a major transcription error — for God MUST have written one more Commandment:

XI. Honor Thy Children

"The Eleventh Commandment"

by Karen Taylor-Good & Lisa Aschmann

She hears his heavy breathing in the dark
His footsteps coming closer down the hall
She's so ashamed, she's Daddy's secret love
She wants to cry, she wants to die,
But he can't get enough

The bruises on his face will go away
Mom keeps him home from school until they fade
She's sorry he was born and tells him so
He takes it in, he hangs his chin,
He ducks another blow

Did God overlook it?
What ought have been written
The Eleventh Commandment . . . honor thy children

He cries for hours, cries and never stops
He shakes so hard his little cradle rocks
He'll never have the chance to be brand new
He'll never walk, he'll never talk He's addicted too

Did God overlook it?
What ought have been written
The Eleventh Commandment ... honor thy children

Thou shalt not kill, Thou shalt not steal
Thou shalt not take the Lord's name in vain
Thou shalt not cause thy children pain

God does not overlook it ... what ought have been written
The Eleventh Commandment ... honor thy children
Honor thy children.

Love Note

If you are a survivor of child abuse, or any other form of abuse, I honor you for your struggle. I encourage you to find and/or continue to seek support from other survivors, for in their strength you will find your own.

Teenage Mutant Alien Pod Person

I gave birth to my only child on July 22, 1983. My life changed forever. All of a sudden, there was a tiny human being who needed me. I was the most important person in her life. I rocked. I ruled. Her eyes lit up every time she saw me. I was so cool. Then I blinked, and she was six. She still needed me. I was still the most important person in her universe. She loved every outfit I ever brought home for her. I was Mommy. I was cool.

She's seven. She adores me. She's eight, nine, ten. We go camping together with the Brownies. She's so proud of me.

She's eleven. She loves to go to the movies with me, out to eat with me, just to hang. She adores me.

Blink. She's fourteen. Uh oh. What's going on here? Invasion of the Body Snatchers. The Pod People have come and replaced my precious baby. She won't be seen with me. She looks at me with such disdain. "I HATE YOU!!!" she says. But Rachael . . . it's ME . . . Mommy . . . remember? Your best friend . . . remember? Nope. I am stupid, I am clueless. I am NOT cool.

Rachael, my Rachael. I miss you terribly. I ache for you. Where did you go?

"Heart of My Heart"

(Where Did You Go?)

by Karen Taylor-Good & Brenton Roberts

You were my precious child, my baby soft and sweet
You loved to hold my hand, always looked up to me
But life will not stand still and baby's turned 14
One day we're friends, the next we're enemies
I see your growing pains, but it's not just you that hurts
You don't know who I am, and I miss who you were

Where did you go? Will you come back?
I see you changing, and I can't change that
If you're still in there, please let me know
Heart of my heart, where did you go?

I was the smartest mom, I was the very best
Now I embarrass you, now I'm an idiot
You think I'm too damn old to understand your pain
Maybe I am . . . I'd listen anyway
I'll love you 'til the day I die and even after that
What happened to the child who loved me back?

Where did you go? Who's in your skin?
Sometimes I see you, then you disappear again
If you're still in there, please let me know
Heart of my heart, where did you go?

I know this is the way it's meant to be
Doesn't make it any easier on me

Where did you go? Please send me a sign
Sure could use a little peace of mind
I know you're in there, why not come home?
Heart of my heart . . . heart of my heart . . .
Where did you go?

Love Note

If you are currently experiencing a similar situation with your teenager, please know that most often, they come back. Give them the space to grow and go through this horrendous phase. Rachael is nineteen now, and she's asking for my help, for my opinions, she even asked me out to a movie the other night. Hang in there. I know how much it hurts.

Hello??
Is Anybody There?

I believe with all my heart that we each begin our existence with God, and that together we choose what we will experience in this lifetime — who our parents will be, what challenges we will face. I believe that that's why children "remember" God better than adults do.

When I was a child, I used to walk in the desert behind my house in El Paso, and I remember feeling so close to God. I remember feeling safe, and protected, and watched-over. I remember knowing without a doubt that God was right there for me — always. And then I'm not sure what happened. I "grew up," and started doing a lot of thinking, and questioning, and doubting. How could there be such a thing as "God" anyway? Oh come on. Give me a break! That's what ignorant, weak people use as a crutch! So I spent years ignoring God, feeling lonely to my core, feeling unsafe, feeling unprotected. Life is such a frightening place when we think we were just thrown out here with no purpose, no plan, no direction, and no help.

Little by little, inch by inch, with great trepidation and embarrassment, I began to entertain the possibility of God's existence, again, several years ago. Would I ever be able to feel that connection again? Had my years of denial and doubt somehow angered Him, or pushed Him away? I was amazed to find that after all that time, He had never gone anywhere. All I had to do was to open my ears, to open my heart, and my Friend was right there — waiting.

"Friend"

by Karen Taylor-Good & Dan Earl Stewart

I used to climb this oak tree as a child
I'd sit up on that limb and chat with God a while
There was nothing that we couldn't share back then
God and I, we were the best of friends

But the years they pass the way they always do
And we become adults who have so little time, it's true
To spend our precious hours once again
Talking to an old forgotten friend

Friend . . . are you still there
Waiting patiently, and do I dare
Be the child who bared her soul
For hours here on end
And do you still remember me . . . Friend?

Though my youth has passed and can't return
There's an aching in my heart here so strong,
you'd think I'd learn

That friends are not discarded with the past
And so I've traveled here today to ask

Friend . . . are you still there
Waiting patiently, and do I dare
Be the child who bared her soul
For hours here on end
And do you still remember me . . . Friend?

There's a stirring in these old oak leaves
I hear them up above
Are you waiting still
And will you fill my heart again . . . with love . . . .

Friend . . . are you still there
Waiting patiently, and do I dare
Be the child who bared her soul
For hours here on end
And do you still remember me . . . Friend?
I pray you still remember me . . . Friend.

Love Note

Being a nice Jewish girl from El Paso who ended up smack in the middle of the Bible Belt, and who has been fairly severely beaten up by some well-meaning folks therein, I would never presume to tell anyone how or what to believe. AND, what I tell my sweet parents, who do NOT believe in God is — it really doesn't matter. He believes in you!

Gone Too Soon

My nephew Paul was murdered when he was twenty-one years old. I thought my sister Bonnie would never heal — nor could I imagine who could ever help her heal. By the grace of God, she discovered a group called The Compassionate Friends, an international organization for bereaved parents. Talk about some brave folks, and some caring folks, and some wise folks. With their help, my sister began to be whole again, and even to help other parents who were going through the same terrible pain that she had.

In 1998, Bonnie was helping to put together the Compassionate Friend's conference, which was to take place here in Nashville. She asked me if I'd perform. I said, "Of course," and then we started to think about — perform what? We discussed my song "How Can I Help You Say Goodbye," and both realized that it was way too mother specific, and wouldn't really work. I asked Bonnie to give me a few days, to see if anything would come.

The next morning, I was at the Waffle House® with my husband, Dennis, and he was talking to me, and all of a sudden, I began to hear this song. I mean, the whole song — words, music, everything. I borrowed a pen from the waitress, grabbed a napkin, asked Dennis to forgive me, and I just wrote it down. That has NEVER happened to me — before, or since. I firmly believe that Paul and all of the other children who "left too soon" are up there with God, and they sent me this gift, that I might share it with their parents. The song has become somewhat of a "flagship" song for The Compassionate Friends, as well as other groups and organizations. I am honored that it has brought so much healing, and I am honored to be its scribe.

"Precious Child"

by Karen Taylor-Good

In loving memory of my precious nephew
Paul L. Rodgers

In my dreams . . . you are alive and well
Precious child, precious child

In my mind . . . I see you clear as a bell
Precious child, precious child

In my soul there is a hole
That can never be filled
In my heart there is hope
'Cause you are with me still

In my heart, you live on
Always there, never gone
Precious child, you left too soon
And tho' it may be true that we're apart
You will live forever . . . in my heart

In my plans . . . I was the first to leave
Precious child, precious child
But in this world . . . I was left here to grieve
Precious child, my precious child

In my soul there is a hole
That can never be filled
In my heart there is hope
And you are with me still

In my heart, you live on
Always there, never gone
Precious child, you left too soon
And tho' it may be true that we're apart
You will live forever . . . in my heart

God knows I want to hold you, see you, touch you
And maybe there's a heaven and some day I will again
Please know you're not forgotten until then

In my heart, you live on
Always there, never gone
Precious child, you left too soon
And tho' it may be true that we're apart
You will live forever . . . in my heart

Love Note

If you are a bereaved parent, my heart is with you. I cannot imagine any greater pain. My wish for you is that you find comfort and solace with others who have experienced what you have. Remember, you don't have to go through it alone.

(Please see "People Helping People" at the end of this book.)

The Bane of a Women's Existence

To my sisters everywhere — I feel your pain. I understand your torment. I share the humiliation, the degradation, the embarrassment. What did we ever do to deserve this? And yet, at least once a year, there we find ourselves. In the stirrups.

I needed to share my feelings about this torture that we, as women, must undergo from the time we're twelve until the day we die! I went to my smart and funny friends Ruth Hummel and Pam Belford, and we laughed and we roared and we healed as we wrote this song.

"The OBG Why Me Blues"

by Karen Taylor-Good, Pam Belford, & Ruth Hummel

I've been sittin' here in this waiting room
since twenty after nine
I must have read this magazine at least a hundred times
So you think that I would be relieved,
they finally called my name
But I know what's in store for me,
when I'm back in the saddle again!

I got the OBG why me blues,
My feet are in the stirrups,
Wish someone else was in my shoes
He tells me to relax and I say
Come on doc, would you?
I got the OBG why me blues

Oh nurse, who is that masked man?
I can only see his eyes

It's tough to let a stranger take a gander at these thighs!
He's tellin' me some stupid joke, expectin' me to laugh
But I lost my sense of humor when they put me
up here on "the rack"

I got the OBG why me blues,
My feet are in the stirrups,
Wish someone else was in my shoes
How many more years of this?
Please tell me it ain't true
I got the OBG why me blues

Slide down, slide down, move back, move back
You must keep those things in the freezer!
ΛΛΛΛHHHH!!! What the heck was that?

I got the OBG why me blues,
My feet are in the stirrups and
I wish someone else was in my shoes
For this I pay a hundred bucks?
Must be a womb with a view!!!
I got the OBG, why me, why me . . . blues

Love Note

What more can I say?

Much to Celebrate

What a joy this song was to write. Once Jason and I got over being "star-struck" by our new friend Melissa Manchester, we found such a commonality, such a bond. I mean, Melissa is a nice Jewish girl from New York, Jason is a nice Jewish boy from Philly, and I'm a nice Jewish girl from El Paso! And we have, each one, been on a deep, spiritual quest for meaning in our lives. And we have, each one, been blessed with the gift of music to help us in our quest.

Melissa sat down at the piano and began to play this wonderful, funky, fun groove, and the words and the melody spilled forth from the three of us. And what we got, and what we know, and what we want to pass along is this —

that in spite of all that appears to be "bad," and all that appears to be evil and scary, life is such an amazing gift. Life is such a miracle.

Life is meant to be filled with love and peace and trust and kindness, and what we want to share most of all is — LIFE IS GOOD! ! ! ! !

"Life Is Good"

by Karen Taylor-Good, Melissa Manchester, & Jason Blume

When the TV tells me the world is a scary place
I turn it off and tune in to my own space
I hear the truth it comes in loud and clear
I've got everything I need, I've got nothing to fear

Life is good, we're talkin' miracle
Life is good, way past wonderful
Even when it doesn't look the way I think it should
Knock on wood, life is good

So when the stormy clouds fill up the sky
Though you can't see it the sun is shining bright
Your dream is waiting, how far can you reach?
We've got heaven here on earth, go and grab your little peace

Life is good, ain't it beautiful?
Life is good, way past wonderful
Even when it doesn't look the way I think it should
Knock on wood, life is good

Oooooooo . . . I'm gonna celebrate!
Oooooooo . . . feel the joy with every breath I take!

Life is good, it's such a precious gift
Life is good, sure beats the alternative!
Even when it doesn't look the way I think it should
Knock on wood, life is good
Knock on wood, life is good
Knock on wood . . . life is soooooooooooooo good!!!

Love Note

If you are going through a rough patch right now, please find at least ONE thing each day to be grateful for. Even if it's just for being alive! I'm so happy that you are.

This Too Shall Pass

My daughter Rachael informed me recently that she's thinking about moving out of the house. I held it together pretty well as we talked about apartments, mattresses, furniture, and utility bills. Then she went off to work, and I sat on the couch and just lost it. I sobbed at the thought of her not being in the house anymore. I wondered how I would ever get through it, and how anybody ever gets through it. AND, the truth is, children leave.

Last Sunday, I took my parents back to their apartment after dinner and a great game of Password™ (Please picture: the opposing team must put their fingers in their ears as I YELL the password to my dad, who is weak in sight, and quite hard of hearing — and I must always sit next to my mama, so that I can whisper the password to her several times during the game, since she is legally blind and can't see the password, and also can't quite remember it for long!) I was musing about how funny they are, and how dear they are, and how old they are, and that at 89 and 87, it just can't be long before they'll be leaving me, too. The truth is, parents leave.

How does anybody get through life? Why are we not simply a planet of "walking wounded?" How do we survive the losses, the changes? I believe it's because God sends us a very, very special Angel— the most powerful one of all — the one whose powers are tested and proven over and over and over again. And the Angel's name is — "Time." And we are all scooped up and held and rocked and healed in His amazing, loving hands.

"Healing in the Hands of Time"

by Karen Taylor-Good & Lisa Aschmann

He has a gentle salve for the wounded
A pillow for the weary soul
The only hope for some broken hearts
He is time, and he'll make us whole

We're all healing, healing,
Healing in the hands of time
We're all healing, healing,
Healing in the hands of time

He's taking us all on a journey
He knows exactly every inch of this road
And if we could only see farther down it
We would know . . . as he knows, that

We're all healing, healing,
Healing in the hands of time
We're all healing, healing,
Healing in the hands of time

If it's much too big today to handle
Just hand it all over to him
Father Time, the master of surprises
Will surprise us once again

We're all healing, healing,
Healing in the hands of time
We're all healing, healing,
Healing in the hands of time

Love Note

If you're hurting right now, and you can't imagine that the pain will ever ease — please know that it will. You are healing, moment by moment, hour by hour, and day by day. Hang in there. Be gentle with yourself. Remember, you are not alone.

People Helping People

It is comforting to know that there are many wonderful support groups and resources available to us when we are in need. Remember, you are not alone. My work has brought me into contact with these particular organizations who have used my music in some way to support their efforts:

National Hospice and Palliative Care Organization
Committed to improving end-of-life care by profoundly enhancing the quality of life for people dying in America and their loved ones.
www.nhpco.org

The Compassionate Friends
Providing support to families that have suffered the death of a child of any age.
www.thecompassionatefriends.org

The Shaken Baby Alliance
Supporting families and professionals in the fight against Shaken Baby Syndrome.
www.shakenbaby.com

Child Help USA®
Dedicated to meeting the physical, emotional, educational,
and spiritual needs of abused and neglected children.
www.childhelpusa.org

International Rett Syndrome Association
Three-fold mission to provide research awareness
and family support for those whose lives are touched
by Rett Syndrome.
www.rettsyndrome.org

Margaret Ann's Place
A healing center for grieving children & families
www.margaretannsplace.org

The Bullying Project
A community providing support and resources
for bullied people.
www.bullying.org

"On Angel's Wings"
CD CREDITS

Executive Producers
Taylor Sparks, Doug Grau & Debbie Matthews

Keyboards
Ed Tossing, Dennis Burnside, Mike Rojas &
Bob Patin

Piano
on "Real" by: KTG

Drums
Paul Scholton & Wayne Killious

Bass
Scott Merry, Sam Weedman & Bob Burns

Electric Guitar
Jerry Kimbrough & Chris Leuzinger

Acoustic Guitar
Larry Beaird & Sam Weedman

Viola & Cello
Jonathan Yudkin

Fiddle
Larry Franklin

Engineers
Brendan Harkin, Sam Weedman, Jim DeBlanc,
David Buchanan, T. W. Cargile,
Chuck Pfaff & Rob Matson

Studios
Wildwood Studio, Samurai Studio, County Q
& Beaird Music Group, Inc.

Mastering & Editing
Max Hutchinson

Special Thanks
To my precious co-writers — Thank you for sharing
your souls.

To Gerald Arthur — Vocal coach/therapist: I'd be lost
without you.